My World of Geography

ISLANDS

Angela Royston

Heinemann Library
Chicago, Illinois

© 2005 Heinemann Library
a division of Reed Elsevier Inc.
Chicago, Illinois

Customer Service 888-454-2279
Visit our website at www.heinemannlibrary.com

Design: Ron Kamen and Celia Jones
Illustrations: Jo Brooker (p. 13), Jeff Edwards (pp. 28–29)
Photo Research: Rebecca Sodergren, Melissa Allison, and
  Debra Weatherley
Originated by Ambassador Litho
Printed and bound in China by South
  China Printing

09 08 07
10 9 8 7 6 5 4 3 2

**Library of Congress
Cataloging-in-Publication Data**

Royston, Angela.
  Islands / Angela Royston.
    p. cm. – (My world of geography)
  Includes bibliographical references and index.
  ISBN 1-4034-5590-2 (HC), 1-4034-5599-6 (Pbk)
  ISBN 978-1-4034-5590-1 (HC), 978-1-4034-5599-4 (Pbk)
  1. Islands–Juvenile literature. I. Title. II. Series.
  GB471.R69 2005
  551.42–dc22

                            2004003865

Acknowledgments
The author and publisher are grateful to the following for
permission to reproduce copyright material:
p. 4 Getty Images/Image bank; pp. 14, 26 Getty
Images/Photodisc; p. 5 Harcourt Education Ltd.; p. 6
(John Farmer) Ecoscene; pp. 7 (Jon Sparks), 12 (Bob
Krist), 17, 18, 25, 27 Corbis; p. 8 Digital Vision; p. 9
(S. Johnson) FLPA; p. 10 Science Photo Library; p. 11 Still
Pictures; pp. 15 (Dave Marsden), 16 (Robert Harding
World Imagery), 20 (Adrian Muttitt), 21 (Jon Arnold
Images), 24 (Nick Hanna) Alamy Images; p. 19 Robert
Harding Picture Library; p. 22 (Wayne Walton) Lonely
Planet; p. 23 Natural History Photo Library.

Cover photograph reproduced with permission of
Corbis/BSPI.

Every effort has been made to contact copyright holders of
any material reproduced in this book. Any omissions will
be rectified in subsequent printings if notice is given to the
publisher.

Contents

Some words are shown in bold, **like this.** You can find out what they mean by looking in the glossary.

What Is an Island?

An island is an area of land that is surrounded by water. Sometimes islands are in lakes and rivers, but most islands are in the sea or ocean.

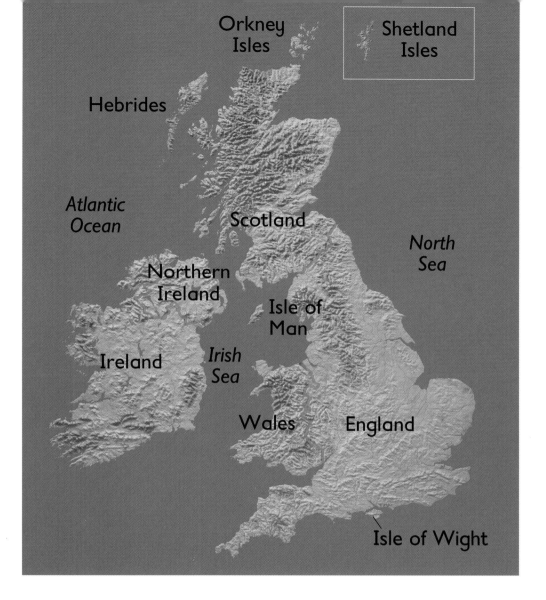

Islands can be big or small. This map shows the British Isles. The British Isles are made up of two big islands and many smaller islands.

Pieces of Mainland

Some islands are pieces of **mainland** that have been cut off by the sea or a river. The water wore away the land between the island and the mainland.

This island used to be part of the mainland. The sea wore away the rocks between the island and the mainland.

Sometimes the level of the sea rises. Seawater then covers large areas of low land. What used to be the top of a hill or mountain becomes an island.

Oceanic Islands

Some islands are the tops of high mountains or **volcanoes** that rise up from the bottom of the sea. They are called **oceanic islands.**

*This photo shows the coast of one of the Hawaiian Islands in the Pacific Ocean. The rocks are made of black **lava** from the volcano that formed the island.*

The island of Surtsey in Iceland rose out of the sea in 1963.

Surtsey is a **volcanic** island that rose up near the **coast** of the country of Iceland. Some volcanic islands are still **erupting.** Others stopped erupting long ago.

Coral Islands

Coral islands are made by millions of tiny sea animals called coral **polyps.** Coral polyps live in warm, **shallow** seas.

When a coral polyp dies, its **skeleton** remains. New coral polyps live on top of the skeletons. Over hundreds of years, the coral builds up to form an island.

Florida Keys

The Florida Keys are a line of small **coral** islands. The word *key* means "small island." Some of the islands are joined together by road bridges.

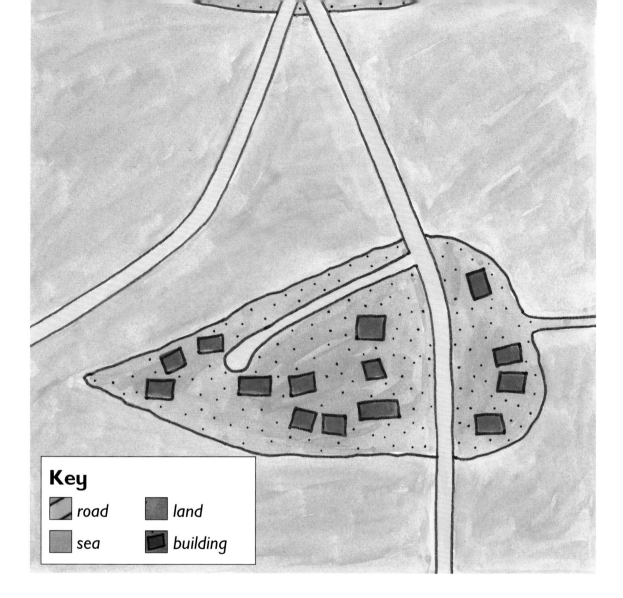

Key

- road
- sea
- land
- building

This map shows the same island as the photo on page 12. It also shows the roads that join one island to the next. You could draw a map like this.

Wildlife

The plants and animals on most islands are the same as those on the nearby **mainland.** Islands without many people may become safe places for seabirds and other animals.

The animals on this island beach are elephant seals.

Some islands have plants and animals that are different from anywhere else in the world. **Tuataras,** like this one, live only in New Zealand.

Farming and Fishing

People who live on islands often get some of their food from farming. They grow **crops** and keep animals, such as sheep and goats.

Islands are surrounded by water, so
islanders can get food from fishing.
Some islanders earn money by
working for **tourists.**

Island Cities

Some cities are built on islands. Many people live on the small island of Hong Kong. The island has lots of tall buildings.

Some cities started on an island but spread on to the **mainland.** Manhattan is an island in the Hudson River. It is also the center of New York City.

Traveling to Islands

You have to travel by boat or **hydrofoil** to reach most islands. Ships carry people, cars, and things like food and clothes to islands. Hydrofoils carry people.

Often, the quickest way to reach an island is by airplane. Planes carry **tourists** to and from islands where there are airports.

Stopovers

Islands are useful places to stop during long journeys across the ocean. People sailing ships stock up on fresh water and food before they continue their journeys.

Island **ports,** like this one in the Azores Islands near Portugal, have been used by ships for hundreds of years.

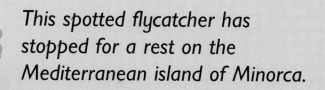

This spotted flycatcher has stopped for a rest on the Mediterranean island of Minorca.

Some birds make long journeys, flying across seas and oceans. They may stop on islands for a short time to rest and wait for good weather.

Enjoying Islands

People often like to go to islands for vacations, particularly when the weather is hot. **Tourists** enjoy spending time on beaches and swimming in the sea.

Easter Island in the Pacific Ocean is hard to get to. Tourists visit the island so they can see these huge stone statues.

All islands are different. Tourists can travel around an island to see the different plants and animals. They might also visit famous buildings or other places.

Spoiling Islands

Some islands are being spoiled by people. Large hotels and airports are built for **tourists.** Sometimes these buildings destroy beautiful parts of the island.

People visit **tropical** islands to see the **coral reefs.** But reefs are easily damaged by boats and divers who break off pieces of **coral.**

Islands of the World

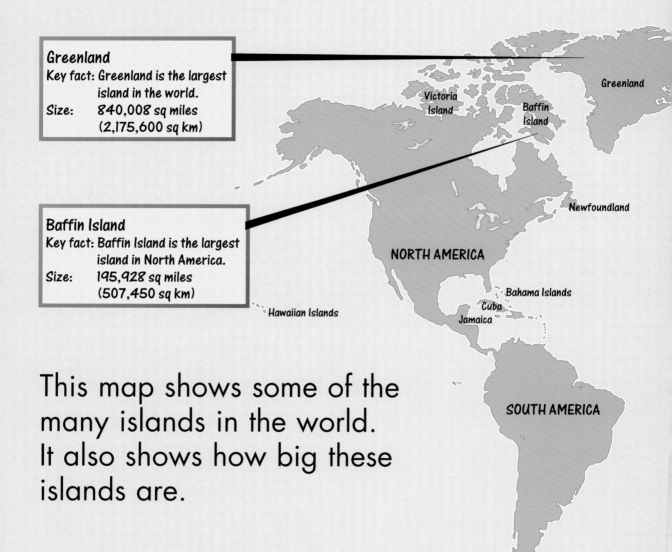

Greenland
Key fact: Greenland is the largest island in the world.
Size: 840,008 sq miles (2,175,600 sq km)

Baffin Island
Key fact: Baffin Island is the largest island in North America.
Size: 195,928 sq miles (507,450 sq km)

Greenland

Victoria Island

Baffin Island

Newfoundland

NORTH AMERICA

Bahama Islands

Cuba

Jamaica

Hawaiian Islands

SOUTH AMERICA

This map shows some of the many islands in the world. It also shows how big these islands are.

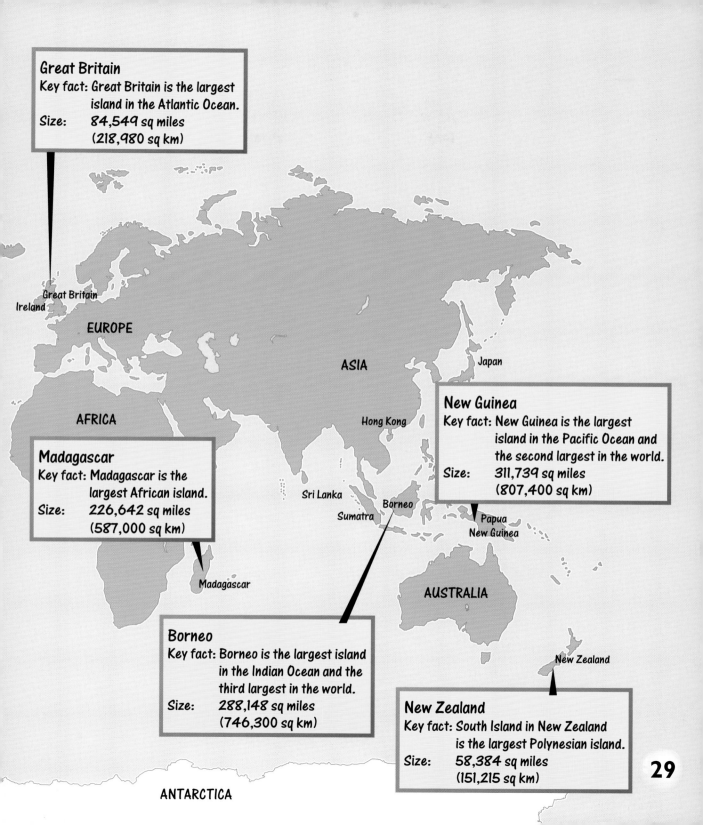

Great Britain
Key fact: Great Britain is the largest
island in the Atlantic Ocean.
Size: 84,549 sq miles
(218,980 sq km)

Great Britain

Ireland

EUROPE

ASIA

Japan

AFRICA

Hong Kong

New Guinea
Key fact: New Guinea is the largest
island in the Pacific Ocean and
the second largest in the world.
Size: 311,739 sq miles
(807,400 sq km)

Madagascar
Key fact: Madagascar is the
largest African island.
Size: 226,642 sq miles
(587,000 sq km)

Sri Lanka

Sumatra

Borneo

Papua
New Guinea

Madagascar

AUSTRALIA

Borneo
Key fact: Borneo is the largest island
in the Indian Ocean and the
third largest in the world.
Size: 288,148 sq miles
(746,300 sq km)

New Zealand

New Zealand
Key fact: South Island in New Zealand
is the largest Polynesian island.
Size: 58,384 sq miles
(151,215 sq km)

ANTARCTICA

29

Glossary

coast land along the edge of the sea

coral hard substance made from the skeletons of tiny animals. A coral reef is a ledge made of coral that lies just underneath the seawater.

crop plant grown for food

erupting exploding or bursting out

hydrofoil boat that skims over the water

islander person who lives on an island

lava hot, melted rock that erupts from a volcano

mainland main part of a country or continent, as opposed to an island

oceanic island island far out in the ocean

polyp kind of animal with a hollow, cylinder-shaped body that lives in the sea

port town or city where ships load and unload

shallow not deep

skeleton bones or shell of an animal

tourist person who visits a place on vacation

tropical coming from hot, wet places on or near the Equator

tuatara type of lizard that lives only in New Zealand

volcano place where lava escapes through a hole in the ground. When something is volcanic, it means that it was caused or made by a volcano.

More Books to Read

Ashwell, Miranda, and Andy Owen. *Seas and Oceans*. Chicago: Heinemann Library, 1998.

Galko, Francine. *Coral Reef Animals*. Chicago: Heinemann Library, 2003.

Galko, Francine. *Sea Animals*. Chicago: Heinemann Library, 2003.

Galko, Francine. *Seashore Animals*. Chicago: Heinemann Library, 2003.

Llewellyn, Claire. *Coral Reefs*. Chicago: Heinemann Library, 2000.

Llewellyn, Claire. *Islands*. Chicago: Heinemann Library, 2000.

Winne, Joanne. *Living on an Island*. Danbury, Conn.: Scholastic Library, 2000.

Index